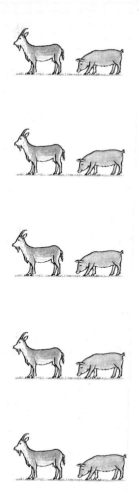

This book is the property of

Haberdashers' Aske's School for Girls

Infant Library Bus

A DORLING KINDERSLEY BOOK

Senior Editor Jane Yorke
Editor Dawn Sirett
Senior Art Editor Mark Richards
Art Editor Jane Coney
Production Marguerite Fenn

Photography by Philip Dowell
Additional Photography by Michael Dunning
(pages 10-11 and 14-17)
Illustrations by Martine Blaney,
Dave Hopkins, and Colin Woolf
Animals supplied by Ashdown Forest Farm,
Hackney City Farm, Horton Park Farm,
and Surrey Docks Farm

Eye Openers ®

First published in Great Britain in 1991
by Dorling Kindersley Limited,
9 Henrietta Street, London WC2E 8PS
Reprinted 1991

A CIP catalogue record for this book is
available from the British Library.

ISBN 0-86318-457-X

Reproduced by Colourscan, Singapore
Printed and bound in Italy by L.E.G.O., Vicenza

Farm Animals

DORLING KINDERSLEY
London ⸱⸱⸱⸱⸱ gart

Cow

horns

Farmers milk their cows every day, so that we have fresh milk to drink. A baby cow is called a calf. A calf sucks milk from its mother's udder. Cows live out in the fields. They eat a lot of grass.

moo

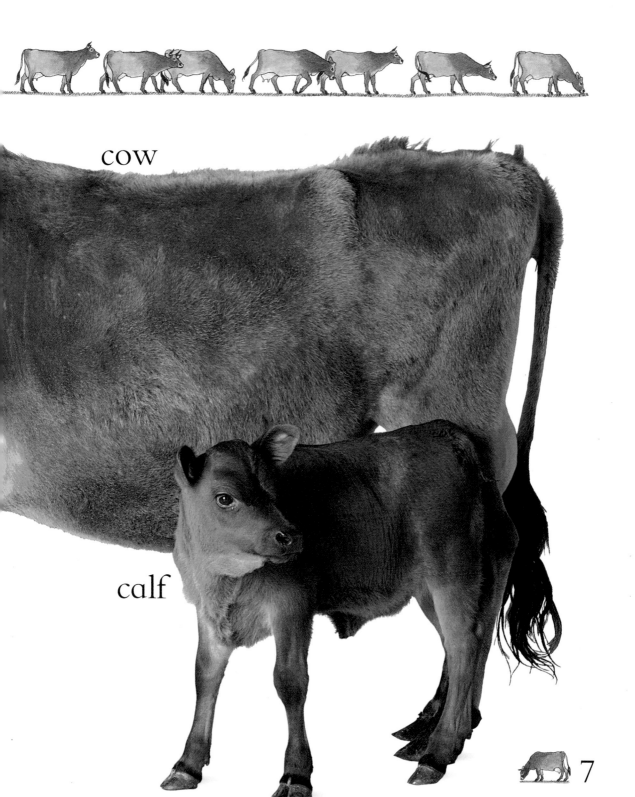

cow

calf

7

Sheep

A mother sheep is called a ewe. A ewe has her lambs in the springtime. In early summer farmers shear their sheep. The winter coats are spun into wool.

ewe

baa

tail

lamb

9

Chicken

A mother hen lays her eggs and sits on them to keep them warm. Fluffy yellow chicks hatch from the eggs after three weeks. The hen teaches her chicks to peck the ground to look for food.

cheep, cheep

chick

hen

11

Pig

A mother pig is called a sow. She has about 14 piglets at a time. Some pigs live indoors in a pigsty. Others are kept outdoors. When it's hot, they lie down in wet mud to keep cool.

oink, oink

sow

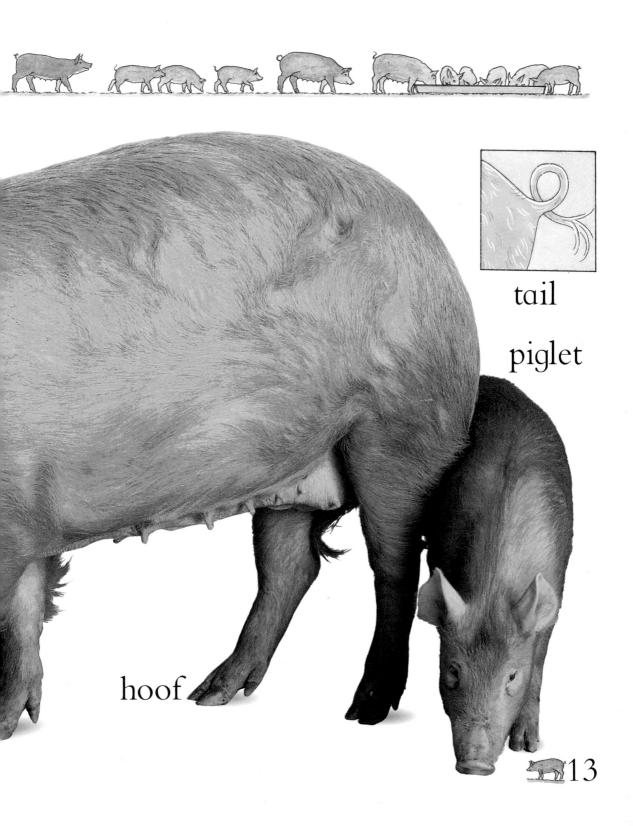

tail

piglet

hoof

13

Horse

Some farmers keep work horses to pull heavy carts and machinery. Other farmers have horses for riding. A horse wears metal shoes to protect its hooves. A blacksmith nails on the shoes, but it does not hurt the horse.

neigh

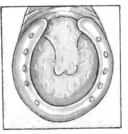

hoof

14

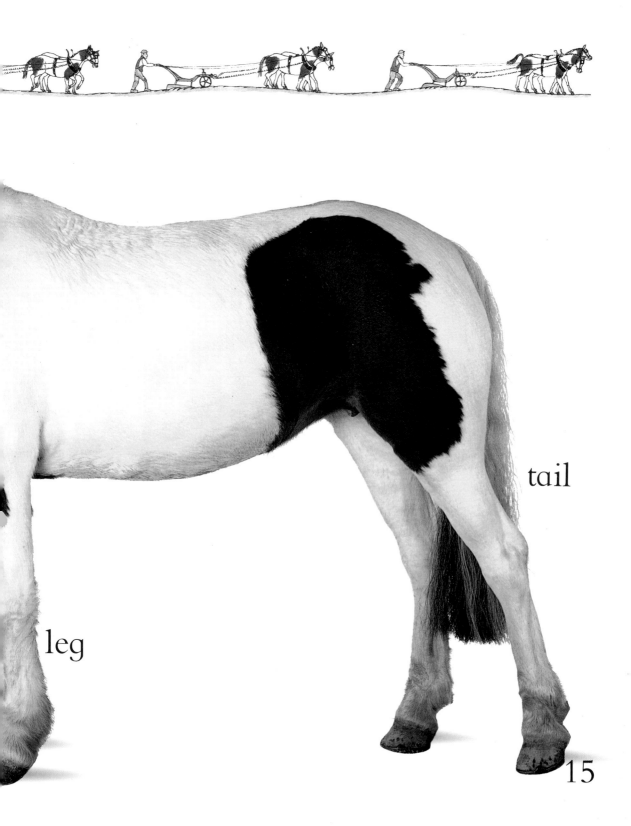

tail

leg

15

Duck

Ducks usually live
near the farmyard pond
or stream. They search
for food in the water.
Ducks eat worms,
waterweeds, and seeds.
A young duck is
called a duckling.

ducklings

duck

foot

quack, quack

tail

17

Goat

A mother goat is called a
nanny goat. Farmers milk
their nanny goats. The
milk is usually turned into
cheese. Young goats are
called kids. Kids playfully
butt and chase each
other around the fields.

nanny goat

beard

kid

meh, meh

udder

19

Sheepdog

Sheepdogs work hard for the farmer. They help round up sheep and other animals into pens. The dogs are trained to obey the farmer's calls and whistles.

ear

tail

paw

woof

21

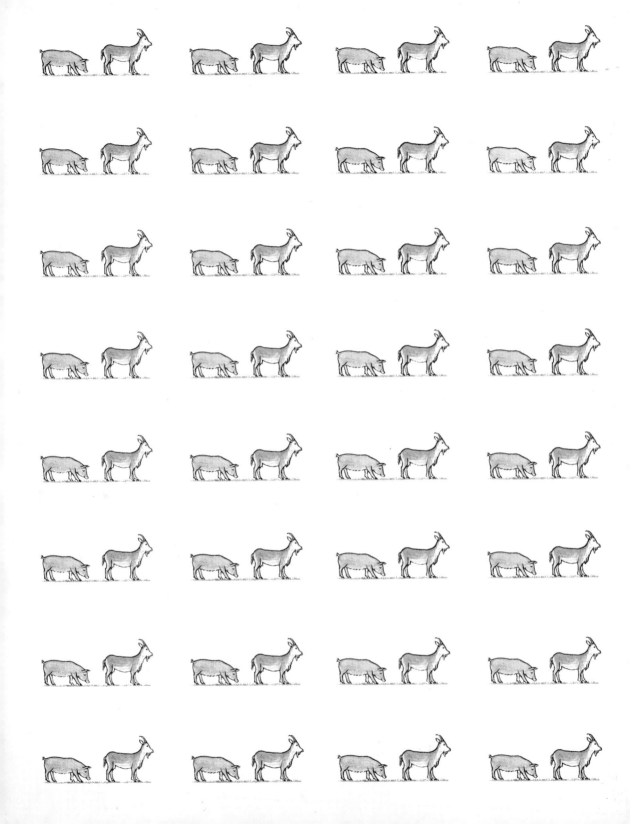

The life cycle of a
Cat

Ruth Thomson

WAYLAND

First published in 2006 by Wayland
an imprint of Hachette Children's Books

British Library Cataloguing in Publication Data
Thomson, Ruth
  The life cycle of a cat. - (Learning about life cycles)
  I. Cats - Life cycles - Juvenile literature
  I Title
  571.8'19752

Editor: Victoria Brooker
Designer: Simon Morse
Senior Design Manager: Rosamund Saunders

Printed and bound in China

Hachette Children's Books
A division of Hodder Headline Limited
338 Euston Road, London NW1 3BH

Photographs: Cover main image, 4–5 Blickwinkel/
Alamy; 2 Ulrike Schanz/naturepl.com; 6, 7, cover
inset centre, 16, 22, 23 Aflo/ naturepl.com; 8, 23
Bartussek/ ARCO/ naturepl.com; 9, 10, 12, 13,
14, 15, 17, 18, 23 Jane Burton/naturepl.com;
cover inset top, cover inset bottom, 11, 19,
23 Wegner/ ARCO/naturepl.com; 20 and 21
Bengt Lundberg/naturepl.com

ISBN-13: 978-0-7502-4865-5
ISBN-10: 0-7502-4865-3

Contents

Cats live here

Most cats live with people in their homes. People feed and look after cats and give them a warm place to sleep.

What is a cat?

Pet cats belong to the animal family that includes wild cats such as lions. All cats are meat eaters. They can run fast or **stalk** silently on their soft **paws**.

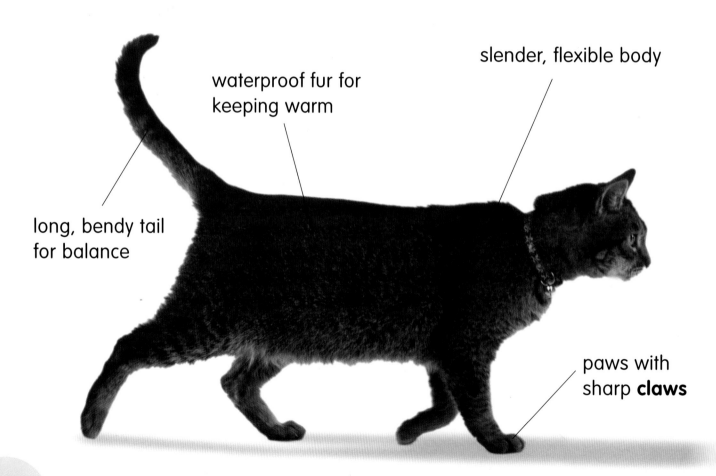

slender, flexible body

waterproof fur for keeping warm

long, bendy tail for balance

paws with sharp **claws**

Cats have very sharp senses.

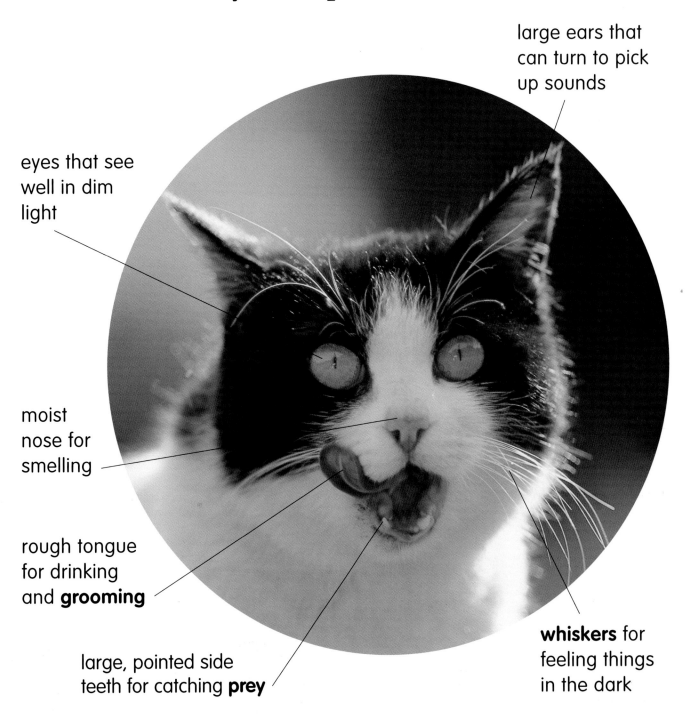

large ears that can turn to pick up sounds

eyes that see well in dim light

moist nose for smelling

rough tongue for drinking and **grooming**

large, pointed side teeth for catching **prey**

whiskers for feeling things in the dark

Birth

A mother cat gives birth to a **litter** of four or five kittens. The newborn kittens are tiny and damp. Their mother licks them dry.

A newborn kitten is weak
and helpless. It cannot see
or hear, and it has no teeth.

Its legs are floppy and its **claws**
stick out from its **paws**.

Baby kittens

The kittens snuggle up to their mother to keep warm. They **suckle** on her milk. Each kitten chooses a **teat** and always suckles on the same one.

1 day

1 week

The mother begins to leave
her kittens for a short while. The kittens
sleep in a heap. They keep each other
warm while their mother is away.

11

10 days

Walking

After a week or so, a kitten's eyes and ears open. But it takes a few more days before the kitten can see or hear well. It can crawl about, but wails if it cannot find its mother.

Soon the kitten is strong
enough to stand and take
its first steps.

3
weeks

Growing up

The kittens begin to grow teeth. Then they can start eating kitten food and drinking water.

4 weeks

The kittens become very curious.

They sniff everything.

They tap objects.

They have play-fights.

Learning

The kitten learns from its mother
how to **groom** itself. It licks its front
paw and wipes it across its face
and ears. It twists its head to groom
the side of its body.

The mother cat helps her kittens learn hunting skills.
She waves her tail as if it were a moving **prey**. The kittens **stalk** and pounce on it.

8 weeks

Playing

The kittens become bolder
and stronger. They love playing.
They watch a toy on a string
and leap into the air
to grab it.

9
weeks

The kittens like to climb everywhere. They use their **claws** to grip.

Going outside

As the kittens grow older, they like spending time outside. They climb trees, find sunny spots to sleep and may chase mice or birds.

10 weeks

By six months, the kittens are young cats. They like to wander as they please. They can always find their own way home.

6
months

1
year

Adult cat

Cats are fully grown when they are a year old. Now they can produce kittens of their own.

Cat life cycle

Birth
The mother cat
gives birth to four
or five kittens.

1 week
The kittens spend
all day suckling
or sleeping.

1 year
Cats are fully grown and can
have kittens of their own.

2-3 months
The kittens play, explore and
learn to hunt inside and outside.

23

Glossary

claw a long curved, pointed nail at the end of an animal's **paw**

groom to clean by licking or pulling through fur

litter a family of baby animals born at the same time

paw an animal's foot

prey the animals that are killed by other animals for food

stalk to hunt an animal quietly trying to keep hidden

suckle to feed on milk from a mother

teat the part of a female animal that its babies suck to get milk

whiskers the long, stiff hairs on the face of a cat

Index